SV

WASHOE COUNTY LIBRARY

3 1235 01725 6335

D0132217

NO LONGER PROPERTY OF
WASHOE COUNTY LIBRARY

A vintage white tablecloth with red poppies is a perfect backdrop for a red plate holding a "love letter". The "US Postal Service" fold is especially nice when the napkin has some lace or embroidery in at least one corner. (See Page 136)

NAPKINS
60 Easy Folds

Simple, Fun & Fancy
All-American Ideas to Decorate Your Table

Written & Illustrated by
Norma Starts

 Turkeyfoot Publishing
Akron, Ohio

Sierra View Library
Old Town Mall
4001 S. Virginia
Reno, NV 89502

Copyright © 1999 by Norma Starts

All rights reserved. No part of this book may be reproduced or transmitted by electronic, mechanical photocopying, recording or any other means or form without permission in writing from the publisher. Exceptions are made for brief excerpts used in published reviews.

Published by Turkeyfoot Publishing
489 W. Turkeyfoot Road, Akron, OH 44319
Phone: 330-645-0373   Fax: 330-645-9801
e-mail: napkinfolder@gwis.com
Order Department: 1-888-335-FOLD (1-888-335-3653)

Manufactured in the Good Old USA

Library of Congress Catalog Card Number 98-90148

ISBN 0-9674465-0-3

This book is available at quantity discounts for bulk purchases. For information, call 1-888-335-3653

Acknowledgments

Heartfelt thanks to Gary Rittenour of "The Art Mooseum", Cuyahoga Falls, Ohio, for his hard work and infinite patience with the cover design, production and layout assistance.

Place setting photography by David Allen Base Photography, Akron, Ohio.

Portrait photo by Drobny Studio, Akron, Ohio.

Printed by Rohrich Corporation, Akron, Ohio.

The sculpted clay "lioness" on page 102 was created by Pat Raeder of "A Way With Clay", Cuyahoga Falls, Ohio. Kitchenware casserole of cast aluminum on page 102 was created by Don Drumm Studios, 437 Crouse Street, Akron, OH 44311.
"Albert", the figurine on page 43, is from Margaret Crunkleton's "Lincoln County Garden Club", PO Box 456, Denver, NC 28037. The "You Are Special Today" red plate on page 2 is from Waechtersbach USA, Inc., 4201 NE 34th Street, Kansas City, MO 64117.

THANKS, THANKS, THANKS, THANKS, THANKS, THANKS, MANY THANKS...

To all the friends who allowed me to raid their cupboards for photo props, provided creative inspiration, technical advice, and endless encouragement: Virginia Whitmore, Barbara Harding, Dad, Marcene Hagarty, Mary June and Dick Starts, Louise and Bill Forsch, Sandy and Ryan Barker, Betty and Carl Cole, Coletta Clermont, Marilee Caswell, Martha Gaskill, Ed Iacona, Carol King, Connie McCurry, Barb Allen, Linda Molnar, and Norma Rist.

For testing, testing and re-testing the fold instructions: Virginia Whitmore, Wanda Garland, Mary June Starts, Barbara Harding, Louise Forsch, Phyllis Tolar, Pat Smith, Barb Wolfe and Bonnie Snyder.

And humble gratitude to everyone else in my life who has stood still long enough to let me talk about this project until the cows came home...

Contents

Also see our Kid's Placemat Patterns and Tabletop Themes on pages 144-150

Introduction

Many years ago a friend gave me a little book on napkin folding that sparked my interest in creating fun tabletop decorations. As I mastered some of the more common folds, it was fun to manipulate those squares of fabric or paper into some original designs too. Collecting old and antique linens and dishes came naturally as I developed different ideas and themes for the table. In 1982 I stumbled across Martha Stewart's book "Entertaining", and her amazing creativity and gorgeous photos further fueled my desire to create a book too.

I believe that families don't spend enough time at the table together in today's society. The communication and learning process that goes on there is priceless. It seems to be a program of attraction rather than promotion. If children have made the napkin rings, colored some placemats or folded the napkins, they are likely to be there to see everyone else's reaction to their handiwork.

I hope you will be inspired by something fun in this book and create special times for the people in your life.

Happy folding,

Norma

*To my Mother, Verna Starts, for passing on to me
her love of homemaking,*

And

To my Dad, Pat Starts, for his love and encouragement.

AIR FORCE B-52

1. Start with flat napkin.

2. Fold into quarters with open points down.

3. Fold right and left sides into center – maintain a point at the top – use an accordion-type fold so that the side points extend beyond the fold.

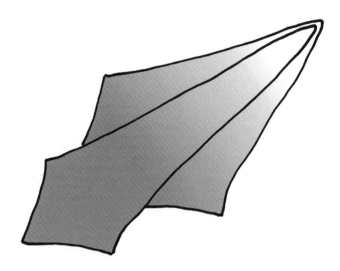

4. Flip the whole thing over.

All-American
ICE CREAM CONE

1. Start with flat napkin.

2. Fold in quarters with loose points at top.

3. Fold the first layer back to the center and tuck inside so it lays flat and forms a pouch.

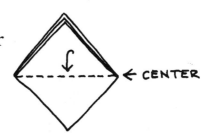

← CENTER

4. Fold next layer back and inside, leaving about an inch exposed.

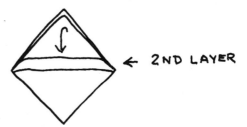

← 2ND LAYER

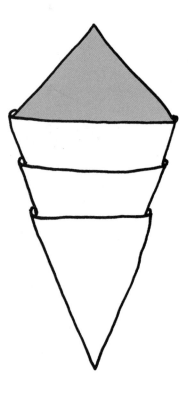

5. Fold next layer back and inside – again leaving about an inch exposed.

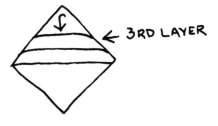

← 3RD LAYER

6. Turn the whole thing over.

7. Fold right and left points into center forming the "cone".

8. Flip back over.

Amber Waves of Grain

1. Start with flat napkin.

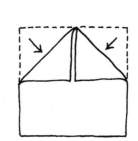

2. Fold top right and left corners down to center of napkin.

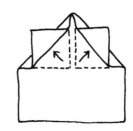

3. Fold the two points that you just brought down to center back up so they extend beyond upper edge.

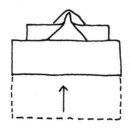

4. Fold up bottom edge to about two inches from top edge of last folds.

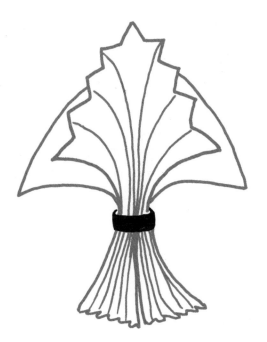

5. Accordion fold from center out to one
    side – then accordion fold the other side
    (Hold the center tightly while folding).

Use a small napkin ring to hold folds together – or use ribbon to tie a bow around the middle – or use natural raffia to tie the center and add a small pine cone for decoration.

ATLANTIC CITY
BREAKERS

1. Start with flat napkin.

2. Fold in quarters with loose points to the right.

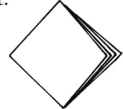

3. Fold bottom up accordion style – most napkins
    will allow only a couple of folds – it should look
    like this with center points towards center:

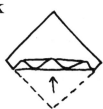

4. Do the same thing with top portion, bringing it down so points touch in center.

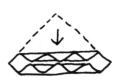

CAN YOU HEAR THE SURF YET?

Place a shell on top of the "waves" (or a posy, acorn, rock – send the kids outside to find something!). This fold will work best with a fabric that creases when pressed down with your fingers so the waves will stay flat.

Blueridge Backpackers

1. Start with flat napkin in diamond position.

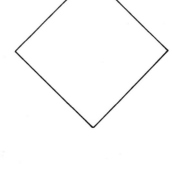

2. Fold bottom up to form triangle.

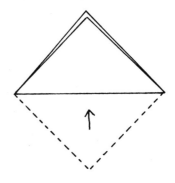

3. Roll each lower corner tightly all the way into the center.

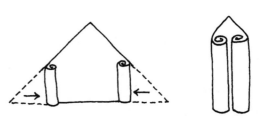

4. Fold in half with points on top and rolls on bottom.

5. Peel top loose layer all the way back and tuck rolls inside (like rolling a pair of socks?).

For a picnic – slip knife and fork into "sleeping bags" or stand it up in a glass and peel back points in front and back.

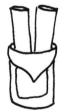

BOISE BAKED POTATO

1. Start with flat napkin.

2. Loosely roll up each side to the middle.

3. Turn whole thing over – smooth side up.

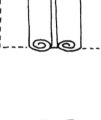

4. Fold top down one-third and bottom up one-third.

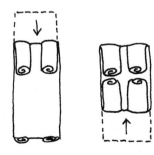

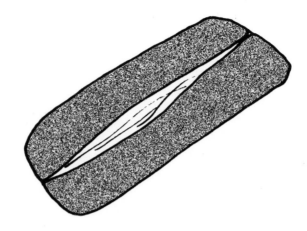

5. Turn it over again and nestle a piece of candy or a pretty flower in the "potato."

ONE HOT POTATO...

Contrast the beautiful soft green of Fire King glassware with bright red flowers and add some sparkle with a darker green glass berry bowl. The napkin fold is the "Ft. Knox Moneybag" with a small grapevine napkin ring embellished with artificial berries. The tablecloth was found in an antique mall and is probably from the 1950's. (See Page 50)

The "Twin Cities" fold really shows off the cute watermelon design on this napkin. A black square plastic plate contrasts with the bright red watermelon placemat that is arranged on a red and white checked tablecloth. A little greenery and a watermelon candle complete this setting. (See Page 132)

*Springtime pastels
coordinated in this setting
enhance the "Jackson Hole Jackrabbit".
I hand-painted this little wooden egg and filled
it with silk tulips for an Easter centerpiece.
Kids love the "bunny" anytime! (See Page 72)*

*A plain black tablecloth
is beautifully contrasted
with the bright sunflowers
in this setting. The cherished
custard glass bell is from
my grandfather's collection.
An "Oahu Orchid" fold
can be placed directly on
the plate as shown or
placed in a stemmed
glass with the lower
"petals" draped over
the outside of the rim.
(See Page 98)*

23

Boston Tea Party

This fold works well with monogrammed napkins or ones with special edging like lace, scallops, printed border or fringe.

1. Start with flat napkin.

2. Fold into quarters with loose points to the top.

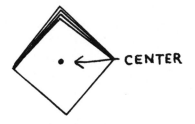

3. Fold the points back to the center.

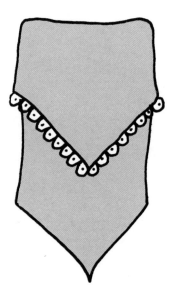

4. Turn the whole thing over – smooth side up – see diagram for position.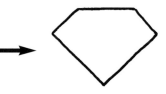

5. Fold left and right corners into center so they overlap.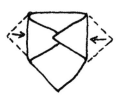

6. Flip over to the right side.

...HOLD THAT "PINKIE" UP!

Bridal Veil
Falls

(Soft, springy fabrics don't work well for this fold.)

1. Start with flat napkin.

2. Fold in quarters with loose points to the right.

3. Accordion fold the top layer back from right to center. (If your napkin is not printed on both sides – accordion fold the top two layers together.)

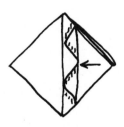

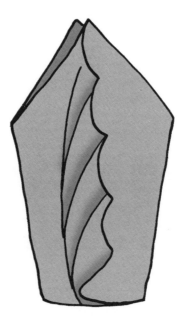

4. Hold on to the center and flip the whole thing over – smooth side up, with loose points to the right.

5. Fold bottom up forming a triangle. The accordion folds should be running up the center.

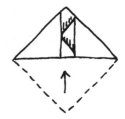

6. Fold right and left points around to form a cylinder, tucking one side inside the other to secure it.

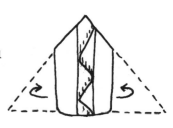

Broadway Bowtie

1. Start with flat napkin.

2. Fold all four corners into the center.

3. Fold top point down to center and bottom point up to center.

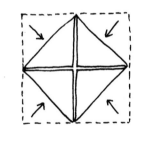

4. Do the same with left and right points.

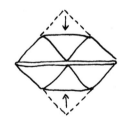

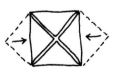

5. Scrunch center together from top to bottom and pull through napkin ring – adjust "bow tie."

This may be too thick to fit through your napkin ring – if so, make your own with a piece of coordinating ribbon or paper – taped together with two-sided tape or glue. Wrapping paper or wallpaper work well too!

CANDLESTICK PARK

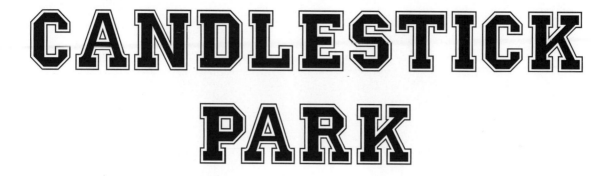

1. Start with flat napkin in diamond position.

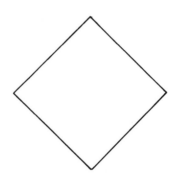

2. Fold bottom point up to top to form a triangle.

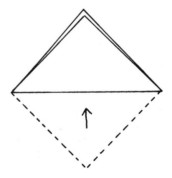

3. Fold top points down about one-third.

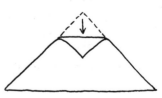

4. Fold top layer (of the part you just folded down) back up toward the top so that it extends above top edge.

5. Fold right side over to within one-half inch of left side. Roll from right to left to form "candle."

This fold will need to be placed in a napkin ring, a glass, or tied with a piece of ribbon at the bottom to hold it together (rough or coarse fabric may stick to itself enough to hold the roll together).

Canyonlands National Park

This fold works best with a stiff napkin.

1. Start with flat napkin.

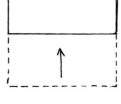

2. Fold in half with open edges on top.

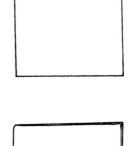

3. Fold top left point down to center of bottom edge and bottom right point up to center of top edge.

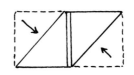

4. Turn the whole thing over.

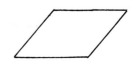

5. Fold top half down to meet lower edge – leaving little triangle on left sticking up.

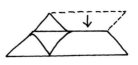

6. Pull the right point from behind and unfold it down per diagram.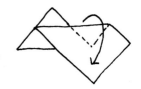

7. Fold the little left triangle in half to the right.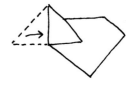

8. Fold up the bottom point.

9. Flip the whole thing over.

10. Fold the left triangle in half and tuck the point inside the right side and then stand it up and shape it into a nice cylinder.

CEDAR RAPIDS SILO

1. Start with flat napkin.

2. Fold in half lengthwise with open edges at bottom.

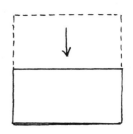

3. Fold in half again.

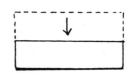

4. Roll loosely forming a cylinder about the size of a small juice glass.

5. Stand on the end with the open edges.

For a slightly different look – roll first part a little crooked – the center will be raised like a cinnamon roll.

CHEYENNE COWBOY

1. Start with flat napkin in diamond position.

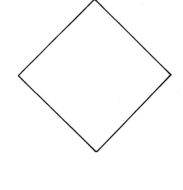

2. Fold into triangle with points down.

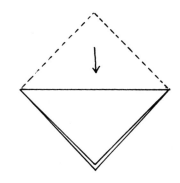

3. Roll tightly starting with bottom points.

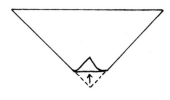

4. Roll all the way to the top to form a cigar shape.

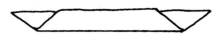

5. Fold in half and pull through napkin ring.

Red or blue "Farmer's Handkerchiefs" create a great effect – Plaids work well too! Use heavy cord or rope if you don't have a napkin ring that coordinates. Or, how about using a "bolo tie"?

Good for a "Chili and Salad Supper"!

Chicago-
The Windy City

1. Start with flat napkin.

2. Gather center together with your fingers.

3. Pick up and place center down into a goblet or pull through a napkin ring.

This fold is great when you are in a hurry!   Swooooosh.

Try placing a printed napkin on top of a lace-edged solid color or use any other two-color combination that appeals to you and complete fold as above.

CHINATOWN FAN

1. Start with flat napkin.

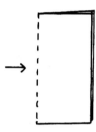

2. Fold in half with open edges to the right.

3. Accordion fold up from the bottom –
   each fold about 1-1/2 inches wide –
   leave top one-fourth unfolded.

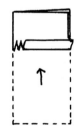

4. Hold securely and flip the whole thing over.

5. Fold in half left to right with the accordion folds on the outside.

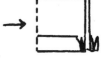

6. Fold down all top right corners of the little square above accordion folds to create a triangle.

7. Turn so the triangle forms a "stand" and the accordion folds fan out to form the "fan."

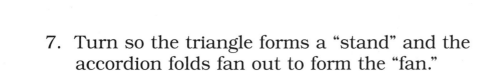

SIDE VIEW

Aaah-so.....

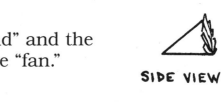

41

Cereal, juice and a croissant will be very inviting when served on this blue Fire King glassware and vintage blue checked tablecloth. The dark red napkin was chosen to match the berry border, then folded into the "Grand Canyon". (See Page 58)

Let the color inspire you! This napkin with its vivid colors just shouted "olé"! It is shaped into the "Saguaro Cactus National Park" fold. The green cactus and little señor are more salt and pepper shakers from my collection. (See Page 116)

42

A red, white and blue theme is great all summer long! Tuck plastic utensils in the "Peoria Picnic Pack" fold and place it on a solid red or blue plate. These copies of antique tomato salt and pepper shakers were found in a gourmet cooking shop. I hand-painted the birdhouse to use as a fun centerpiece. (See Page 106)

The "Greasy Creek, Kentucky Woodpile" is neatly stacked on restaurant-style dishes that belonged to Grandpa Kaufman. He entertained large groups at his home which was built during the depression – hence the name "Depression Ranch" on the dishes. The wonderful character "Albert" sitting on the fence is from Margaret Crunkleton's Lincoln County Garden Club. (See Page 60)

43

DAD'S FORT MYERS SPECIAL

1. Take one full size paper towel.

2. Fold in half (sort of).

3. Tuck under edge of plate (on either side).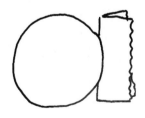

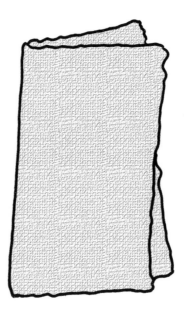

If towel rips – repair it with standard gray duct tape on the underside.

This fold is dedicated to my Dad who "WOWS" the folks at Riverwoods Plantation with it every winter.

FOUR CORNERS

It's easy if you do __every__ step!

1. Start with flat napkin.

2. Fold each point into the center.

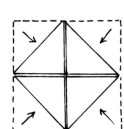

3. Hold securely and flip over.

4. Fold each point again to the center.

5. Hold on and flip over again.

6. Fold each point AGAIN to the center.

7. Hold on and flip over AGAIN.

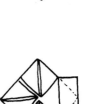

8. Lift each point from the center to form four little cuffs.

This fold makes a nice "coaster" for a chilled bottle of wine – or – put the folded napkin on a plate and place a flower in the center.

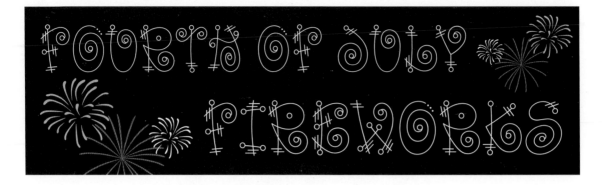

FOURTH OF JULY FIREWORKS

1. Start with flat napkin.

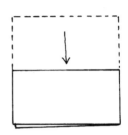

2. Fold in half with open edges at bottom.

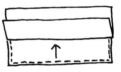

3. Fold the top layer back up to about one inch from top edge.

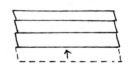

4. Fold bottom layer up to about one inch from top edge of last fold.

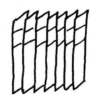

5. Accordion fold from left to right.

48

6. Holding lower edge securely – pull out the top edge of the middle and lower rows - creating two horizontal ruffles.

Place in a napkin ring or glass.

GREAT FAMILY PROJECT: PLASTIC NAPKIN RINGS
Cut 1-1/2 to 2 inch lengths of white plastic plumbing pipe – use glue to attach silk flowers, stars, flags or bows to coordinate with your tabletop theme.

FT. KNOX MONEY BAG

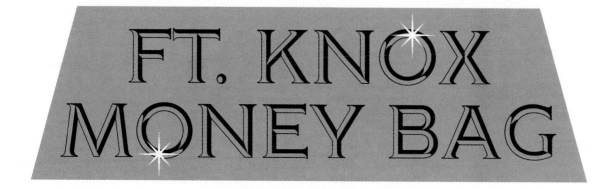

1. Start with flat napkin.

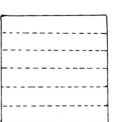

2. Accordion fold from bottom to top.

3. Leave three or four inches lying flat to form base and fold right and left ends up to center to create appearance of a "bag."

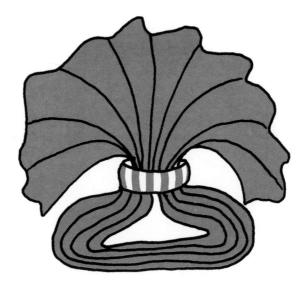

Tuck fun items into center of folds – use a weighted helium balloon, a flag, plastic knife, fork, spoon, or a pretty flower.

DO YOU HAVE A BOY SCOUT OR GIRL SCOUT IN YOUR FAMILY?
Use rope or cord to make napkin rings with a decorative knot. (Possible Mother's Day gifts for the whole troop to make?)

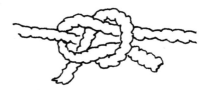

GIANT SEQUOIA

1. Start with flat napkin in diamond position.

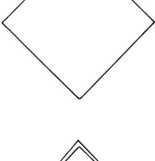

2. Fold into a triangle with points up.

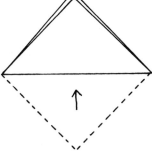

3. Fold up bottom edge about one and one-half inches.

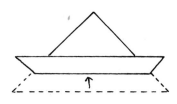

4. Flip the whole thing over.

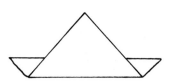

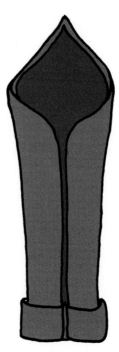

5. Roll left point into center.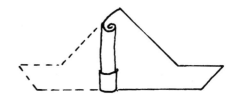

6. Roll right point into center.

Use either side as front – Place in a glass or napkin ring – If the napkin is fairly stiff it will stand on it's own – If the napkin is soft, lay it on the plate or table.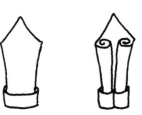

Glacier National Park

1. Start with flat napkin in diamond position.

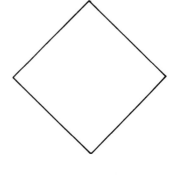

2. Fold into a triangle with points up.

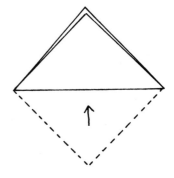

3. Fold right and left points up to the center-top.

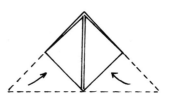

4. Fold bottom point up to about an inch from the top point.

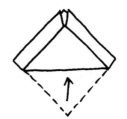

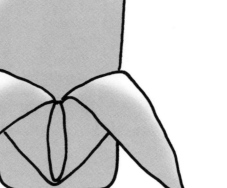

5. Fold that last piece back down to the bottom edge.

6. Flip the whole thing over.

7. Bring right and left sides together and tuck one inside the other to form a cylinder.

8. Turn cylinder around and fold middle, right and left points down.

GOTHAM CITY BAT

1. Start with flat napkin.

2. Fold bottom up one-third.

3. Fold top down to bottom edge.

4. Fold top layer of right and left corners up to form "ears" (bottom center stays down at bottom edge).

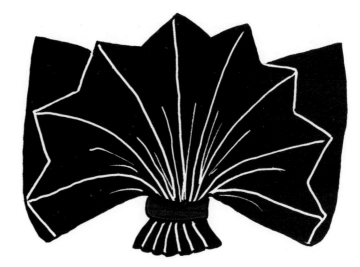

5. Start at left side and accordion fold all the way across.

6. Hold bottom of folds securely and let top fan out. Place the bottom in a napkin ring so it will stand up on a plate or above the plate on the table. Either side can be used as presentation.

Boo!

GRAND CANYON

1. Start with flat napkin.

2. Fold down top one-third.

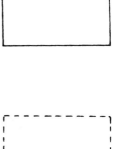

3. Fold the bottom up to the top edge.

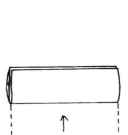

4. Bring right and left sides down to form point at center top.

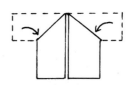

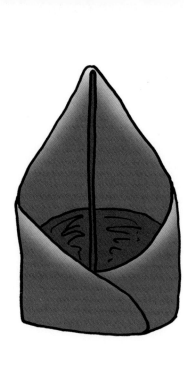

5. Fold up bottom edges of both "legs."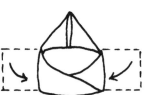

6. Fold right and left sides toward center, tucking one into the other.

7. Form into a cylinder and tuck extra fabric in center down to form bottom of the "canyon."

Use this fold as a holder for a table favor, a flower from the garden, a pine cone, or a dinner roll.

Greasy Creek, Kentucky
WOODPILE

1. Start with flat napkin.

2. Roll the top down to center and the bottom up to the center.

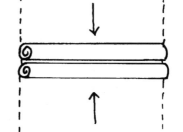

3. Fold right side over to left.

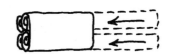

4. Fold the top back to the right side so "logs" are on the top AND fold the bottom under so "logs" are on the bottom.

Use a birdhouse made of twigs for a centerpiece or build a "log" fence around a flower pot using twigs from the yard.

BASIC LINENS
Plain dark green and bright red tablecloths and napkins are the starting point for many of my "creations". Just think how many directions you can go with just these two colors! You have all the major holidays covered and lots of other events too.

Cool, pleasing colors are the basis for this salad setting. Add some crusty bread and lots of crispy fresh veggies for a great salad luncheon. The "Honolulu Bird of Paradise" fold adds just the right touch. (See Page 68)

This unique setting utilizes two contrasting napkins. Fold a green napkin into a triangle and tuck it into a small flowerpot with three "leaves" hanging over the rim. Tuck the "Pottstown Peony" into the center. Use new, clean garden tools to serve a salad. (Check for non-toxic paint on the tools.) This garden setting displays nicely on the ever-versatile dark green tablecloth. (See Page 110)

"An apple a day...."
Primary colors on the apple napkin inspired this setting. I experimented with several different folds to find one that would best display the apple print. The "Las Vegas Pyramid" did the trick! A dark green and white checked tablecloth is another handy basic for your linen closet. The centerpiece includes a birdhouse and hand-painted wooden apple. (See Page 76)

Dark green dishes and napkins are great basic table accents. They are beautiful for Christmas, but work just as well for other times of the year. In this setting, the "Pike's Peak" fold was tied with a red and green plaid taffeta ribbon to create a "Christmas tree". (See Page 108)

63

Hartford Stuffed Cuff

1. Start with flat napkin.

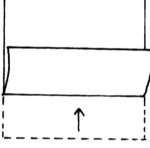

2. Fold bottom up one-third.

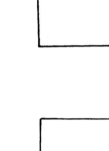

3. Fold top down to within 1 inch of bottom edge.

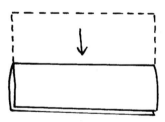

4. Flip the whole thing over.

5. Fold in half lengthwise

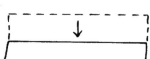

6. Fold left side over toward the right about one-third.

7. Tuck left folded side into "tube" on right side forming a cylinder and shape it into a very neat "shirt cuff."

STICKER FUN
Colorful stickers can be added to plain paper napkins or plastic tablecloths to help develop a particular theme.

HOLLAND, MICHIGAN
TULIP

1. Start with flat napkin in diamond position.

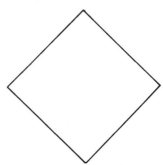

2. Fold into a triangle with points up.

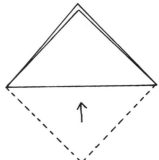

3. Fold right and left points up to the center-top.

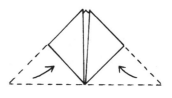

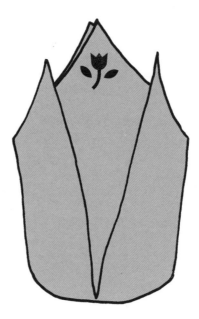

4. Flip the whole thing over with loose points up.

5. Fold bottom point up to the top forming a triangle.

6. Form cylinder tucking right side into left – turn it around and stand it up.

Spring is sprung, the grass is riz,
I wonder where the flowers is!!??

...HERE COMES SPRING!

Honolulu Bird of Paradise

1. Start with flat napkin.

2. Fold in quarters with loose points up.

3. Fold top half down so that all loose points are on top, pointing down.

4. Fold left and right points to the center so they lay flat – they will extend beyond the top.

5. Fold extended parts at top under to the back.

BACK VIEW:

6. Fold in half with split side up and hold blunt end in one hand and lift "petals" up one by one to shape tropical "bird of paradise".

HOLD HERE →

LIFT "PETALS"

DO IT YOURSELF!
Use rubber stamps and colorful ink pads to make plain paper napkins come to life. I found a rubber stamp that has changeable letters and numbers and have used it to make personalized napkins that include names and date of a special event. (Make sure the ink is non-toxic!)

HOUSTON OIL RIG

1. Start with flat napkin in diamond position.

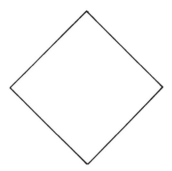

2. Fold into a triangle with points down.

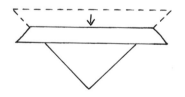

3. Fold the top edge down about one and one-half inches.

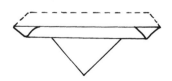

4. Fold down again one and one-half inches.

5. Fold left and right sides in to form "oil rig" legs.

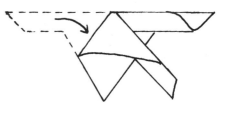

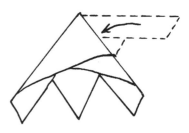

6. Flip the whole thing over and place on plate.

JACKSON HOLE JACKRABBIT

1. Start with flat napkin in diamond position.

2. Fold bottom up to form triangle with points at top.

3. Fold bottom edge up about two or three inches (more if your napkin is large).

4. Fold right and left sides up to the center-top forming a diamond with "ears."

5. Fold the bottom up to form a triangle with "ears."

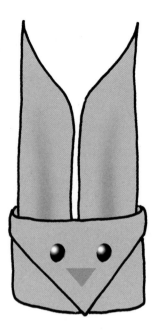

6. Fold the top point of that last triangle back down to the bottom edge.

7. Flip the whole thing over.

8. Fold top point of triangle down to bottom edge.

9. Flip the whole thing over again.

10. Tuck one side into the other to form a small cylinder and turn it around to meet the "jackrabbit."

L.A. Freeway

1. Start with flat napkin.

2. Fold in quarters with loose points in upper right corner.

3. Fold top layer towards center diagonally approximately three times to form first "lane".

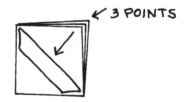

← 3 POINTS

4. Repeat with next layer, folding down 2 or 3 times until second "lane" is parallel to the first.

← 2 POINTS

5. Hold securely and flip the whole thing over.

6. Fold 1/3 of top and bottom toward center and flip back over with "lanes" on top.

DRIVE SAFELY!!!!

LAS VEGAS PYRAMID

This fold works best with a stiff napkin. It also works well with a napkin that has a border print or fringe.

1. Start with flat napkin in diamond position.

2. Fold into triangle with points up.

3. Fold right and left corners up to center-top point.

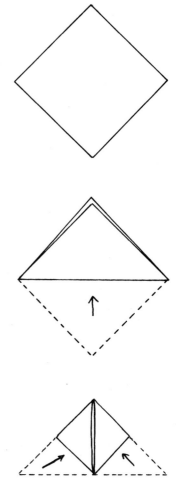

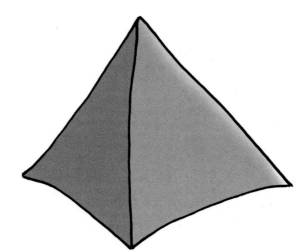

4. Flip the whole thing over.

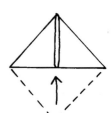

5. Fold bottom point up to the top point, forming a triangle.

6. Hold on and flip over again, with loose points at top.

7. Lift from bottom center so that it forms a two-sided pyramid.

8. Carefully fold the two loose sides forward so they fill the open third side – one piece will fold over on top of the other.

LUBBOCK LONGHORN

1. Start with flat napkin.

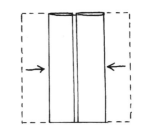

2. Fold right and left sides in so they meet in the center.

3. Fold out each corner diagonally (hold the center down).

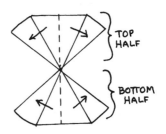

4. Roll the top half tightly down to the center.

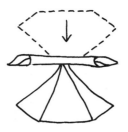

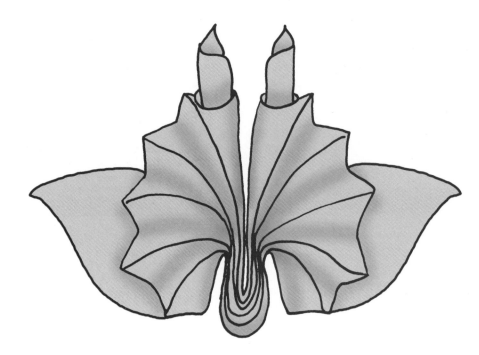

5. Continue holding the rolled portion and accordion fold the remainder down to the bottom edge.

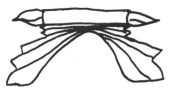

6. Fold in half with the rolls on top and place in a glass or a large napkin ring.

GIT ALONG LITTLE DOGIES...

MOON OVER MIAMI

1. Start with flat napkin.

2. Fold in half with open edges to the right.

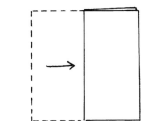

3. Accordion fold from the bottom up to the top, making folds about one inch wide.

4. Slip an elastic ponytail holder or small rubberband over the ends and slide it to the center.

80

5. Fan out accordion folds into a "moon" and place on the plate.

Look for ponytail holders that will coordinate with your napkins. Also, try a small ribbon tied tightly in the center (use a spring-type clothespin to hold the accordion folds while you tie the bow).

This easy fold, called "Rocky Mountain High", is one that is used frequently by restaurants. It is handy for large parties because it can be folded and stacked ahead of time. I found this one and only plate at a flea market and haven't found another one since. The deep blue carnation pattern complements the design and color on the very old pitcher and covered bowl. (See Page 114)

The "Gotham City Bat" fold is perfect for Halloween. It would look just as cute using a black napkin. Little stacked pumpkins are salt and pepper shakers. I use the small black plates frequently – almost any dessert looks special against the shiny black surface. (See Page 56)

82

This setting is very special to me. My Grandma Katie Kaufman embroidered the tablecloth. The calling card that is tucked into the "St. Petersburg Surf" fold was Grandpa Ezra Kaufman's. The calling card is reminiscent of his sense of humor and proclaims him to be "a millionaire's only son, single and out for a good time". The brown and white transferware dishes are favorite pieces from my collection. (See Page 126)

Gold-rimmed plates make a great showplace for the "Bridal Veil Falls". This fold displays the gold stripes that are printed on the green napkins. Try turning printed napkins different directions. The results can be very surprising! I painted this turkey and placed him on a bed of autumn leaves and basket filler. You can also use indian corn, gourds, pumpkins or pine cones in place of the turkey. (See Page 26)

MOUNT RUSHMORE

1. Start with flat napkin.

2. Fold in half with open edges at the bottom.

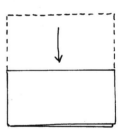

3. Determine the center point of top edge.

CENTER

4. Bring top layer of lower left corner over to the lower right corner – forming a triangle.

I LAYER

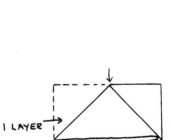

5. Flop the top layer of the lower right corner back to the lower left corner (there are now two triangles on the left side).

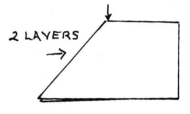

6. Bring the lower top layer of the lower right corner over to the lower left corner (there are now three triangles on the left side).

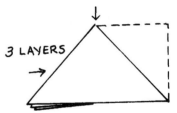

7. Bring the last lower right corner over to the lower left corner – Do you have four triangles on the left side? Yippeeee!

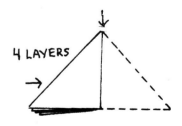

8. Carefully stand it up, fanning out the four triangle folds.

MOUNT ST. HELENS

1. Start with flat napkin in diamond position.

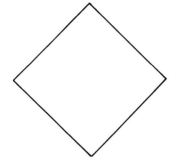

2. Fold up bottom point about four inches (do less if napkin is smaller).

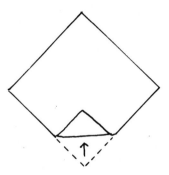

3. Fold bottom up again about four inches.

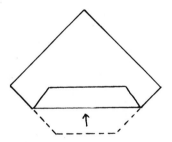

4. Fold again about four inches.

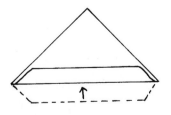

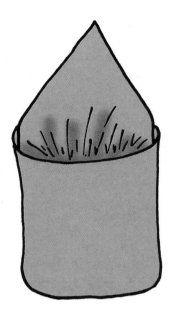

5. One more time!

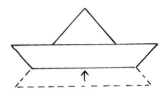

6. Turn the whole thing over.

7. Roll right and left sides into center so that they meet.

8. Turn it around and stand it up so "explosion" is coming out of the mountain.

NEW ORLEANS FLEUR-DE-LIS

Use only napkins that are printed on both sides.

1. Start with flat napkin in diamond position.

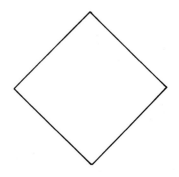

2. Fold into triangle with points down.

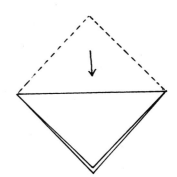

3. Fold up the bottom points so they extend beyond the folded edge.

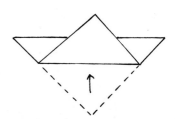

4. Accordion fold left to right.

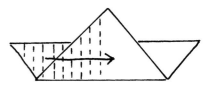

5. Hold the bottom edge of accordion folds securely and place in glass – arrange the side "petals" and then peel one of center points down in the front.

COLOR COORDINATED NAPKIN RINGS
Save leftover scraps or recycle used ribbon - cut into 6″ lengths - tape ends together with two-sided tape.

NEWPORT SAILOR

1. Start with flat napkin.

2. Fold top half down with open edges at bottom.

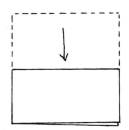

3. Fold right bottom corner up to the center of top edge.

4. Fold top right corner over to left top corner.

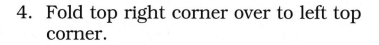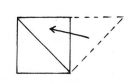

5. Fold top right corner down to form a triangle.

6. Find the center of the left edges (there will be two folded edges and four hemmed edges – pick the center). Open and fold the edge up about two inches all the way around to form the "boat."

NEW RIVER RAFT

1. Start with flat napkin.

2. Fold the top down one-third.

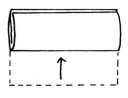

3. Fold the bottom up to the top edge.

4. Fold right and left sides toward center so their top edges meet and form a triangle.

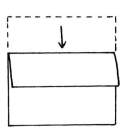

5. Hang on and flip the whole thing over.

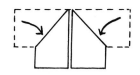

6. Turn up bottom "legs" two times – fold up only to the bottom of the triangle.

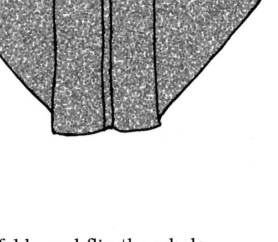

7. Hang on to the folds and flip the whole thing over.

8. Fold bottom up – this is the edge you already double-folded.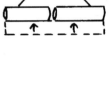

9. Hang on and flip over again.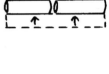

10. Fold bottom right corner up to the center-top.

11. Do the same with the bottom left corner.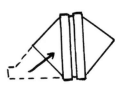

NEW YORK SKYSCRAPER

NEW YORK SKYSCRAPER

1. Start with flat napkin in diamond position.

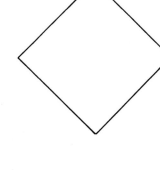

2. Fold into triangle with points up.

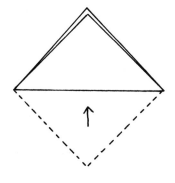

3. Fold up bottom one and one-half inches.

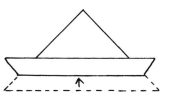

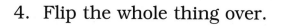

4. Flip the whole thing over.

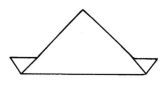

5. Start at left and roll tightly all the way to the other side.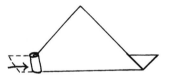

6. Tuck the last one inch or so into the hem to secure it.

Stand it up in a napkin ring or short glass. Do several for a "downtown skyline" centerpiece. Empty votive glasses make nice holders too.

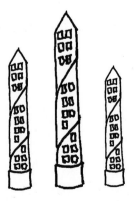

NIAGARA FALLS

1. Start with flat napkin in diamond position.

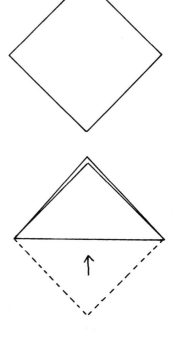

2. Fold into triangle with points up.

3. Fold right and left points up to the top point.

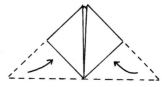

4. Fold bottom point up to about two inches from top and then back down to the bottom edge.

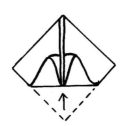

5. Fold top layer (right and left points) down and tuck them underneath top edge of the lower fold.

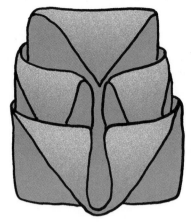

6. There should still be two layers at the top point – Take one layer and fold it down and tuck under the last fold.

7. Hold on and flip the whole thing over.

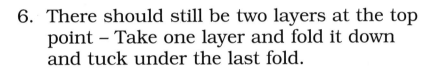

8. Bring right and left corners together and tuck one inside the other creating a cylinder.

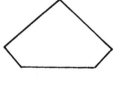

9. Turn around and shape into a nice cylinder, and:
   - display with all points tucked inside the folds, or
   - pull the points out, or
   - pull middle points part of the way out so they "poof."

Oahu Orchid

Use only napkins that are printed on both sides.

1. Start with flat napkin in diamond position.

2. Fold up bottom point to about two inches from the top point.

3. Fold right and left points up to the center top forming a diamond.

4. Fold up the bottom to create a triangle.

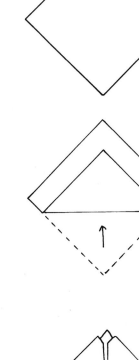

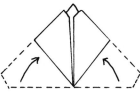

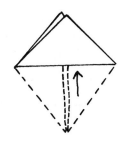

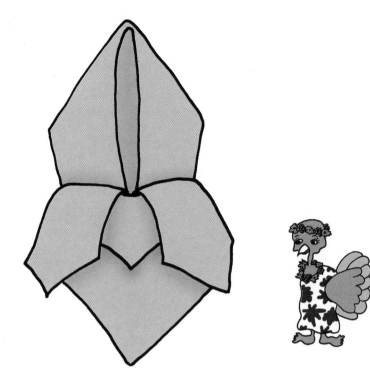

5. Bring right and left points together and tuck one inside the other to form a cylinder.

6. Turn the whole thing around.

7. Hold the bottom with your thumb inside the cylinder and peel back all the points.

PALM BEACH PALM

1. Start with flat napkin.

2. Fold top down about one-third.

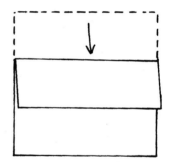

3. Accordion fold from left side all the way to right side.

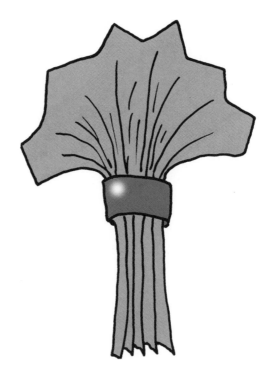

4. Slide a napkin ring on the end that is a single layer and push it up to about the middle. (Press the lower, single-layer portion that will be the "trunk" together tightly with your fingers so that it doesn't fan open).

   Fan open the top end to form the "palm fronds."

Use flat on plate or the table – or – place in a tall glass.

Pink and gray colors are reminiscent of the 1950's. With a classic tablecloth as the background, I used some pink transferware and a beautiful cast aluminum kitchenware casserole by Don Drumm Studios of Akron, Ohio to carry out the theme. The "Boston Tea Party" fold is a great way to display a fringed napkin. (See Page 24)

When I purchased these cotton animal-skin print napkins, I had no idea how dramatic they would be. The black plates with terra cotta rims turned up at a flea market, and then I added bakelite-handled utensils, a basket of jungle greenery and a ceramic "lioness" from Pat Raeder's "A Way With Clay". The fold is called the "Tucson Teepee". (See Page 130)

102

This old, old tablecloth is almost threadbare, but the soft apple green is still a perfect complement for these lime-edged Pyrex dishes. The "Lubbock Longhorn" fold stands up with the help of a square wooden napkin ring. This fold is one that produces really surprising effects with napkins of different styles and designs. (See Page 78)

The 1970's look of this avocado and lime green tablecloth sprinkled with daisies has resurfaced as a favorite color combination today. The "Moon Over Miami" fold fits perfectly on a clear glass salad plate. (See Page 80)

Pasadena ROSE

1. Start with a flat napkin.

2. Fold in half with open edges on the bottom.

3. Start rolling from left side – roll the first turn tightly to form center of "rose".

4. Roll the rest irregularly to form the shape of "petals." The long "stem" can be folded in half or left as is, depending on how you are going to use it. Pinch the fabric and work with your fingers to make a pretty flower after it is in the holder.

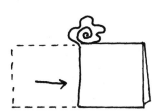

Tuck a green napkin in a deep glass or goblet and then tuck the "rose" in the middle.

Stand "rose" in a long (3") napkin holder – or – sections of sawed off PVC plumbing pipe.

Fold the "stem" portion and stand the "rose" in a juice glass for your breakfast table.

Place several "roses" in a basket - Use plain colored and printed coordinating colors. (This is a nice way to present your napkins for a buffet.)

Peoria Picnic Pack

1. Start with a flat napkin.

2. Fold into quarters with loose points on the top.

3. Roll top two layers together down to the center, forming a belt across the middle.

4. Flip the whole thing over.

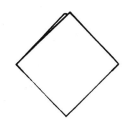

5. Fold right and left points into center.

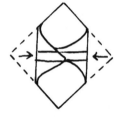

6. Flip back over and use pocket for silverware, a flower, or a note.

BILLY—
GOOD JOB!

Pike's Peak

1. Start with flat napkin in diamond position.

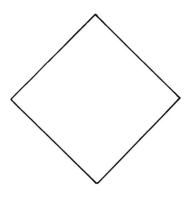

2. Fold into a triangle with points down.

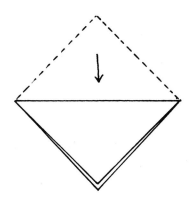

3. Fold left point over to right point to form another triangle.

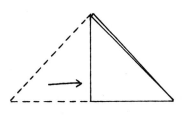

4. Place with open edges at bottom and accordion fold all the way across from left to right.

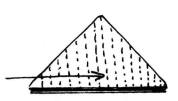

108

5. Hold bottom edge securely and place in glass, goblet, napkin ring, or tie a ribbon into a bow around the accordion folds about two or three inches up from the bottom.

This fold creates a beautiful "Christmas Tree" effect when it is a green napkin tied with a festive holiday ribbon.

POTTSTOWN PEONY

1. Start with flat napkin.

2. Fold into quarters with the loose points on the top.

3. Fold bottom up about three inches.

4. Accordion fold all the way across from left to right.

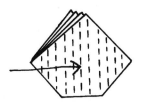

5. Hold the bottom edge securely and place in a glass or small flower pot.

6. Peel the four points apart and then tuck each pointed edge down into the center folds, one at a time, to form the soft "petal puffs".

Fold a green napkin into a triangle and tuck into a flower pot or small basket — let the three points hang out over the edge to create a "leaf" effect and place "peony" in the center.

RENO
FIVE CARD STUD

1. Start with flat napkin.

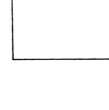

2. Fold into quarters with points down.

3. Fold up the first layer to about one inch from the top point.

4. Do the same with the next three layers – leaving about an inch from the last point each time.

5. Flip the whole thing over – smooth side up.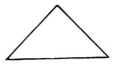

Try these variations:
- ♣ *Turn over and leave as is to lay flat on the table or plate.*
- ♦ *Tuck one side into the other to form cylinder.*
- ♠ *Scrunch together to put into a sturdy napkin ring or a glass.*
- ♥ *Accordion fold left to right, place in a napkin ring, then peel back each point an inch or so.*

Rocky Mountain High

1. Start with a flat napkin in diamond position.

2. Fold into a triangle with points down.

3. Fold down the right and left corners to the bottom point.

4. Turn the whole thing over.

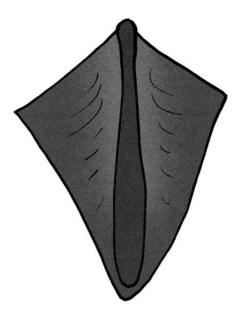

5. Fold top point down to bottom point forming another triangle.

6. Pick up at the center and fold back right and left points so it will stand up.

Either side can face front – pretty with a fringed edge!
This fold is great for a large crowd – they can be folded to step five in advance and stacked.

Saguaro National Monument

1. Start with a flat napkin in diamond position.

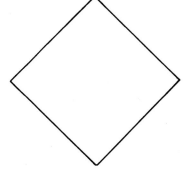

2. Fold into a triangle with points up.

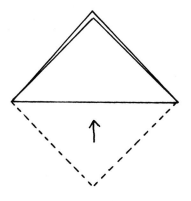

3. Fold up bottom left and right points to center top.

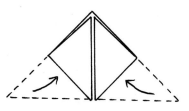

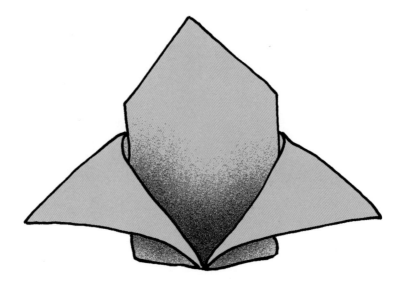

4. Turn the whole thing over – loose points still at the top.

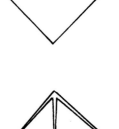

5. Fold up bottom half to form a triangle.

6. Bring right and left points together and tuck one inside the other to create a cylinder.

7. Stand it up, turn it around and fold down the "arms."

San Andreas Fault

1. Start with flat napkin.

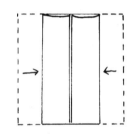

2. Fold right and left sides in so that they meet in the center.

3. Fold in half lengthwise with open edges to the right.

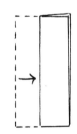

END VIEW

4. Accordion fold from bottom to top, making each fold about one and one-half inches wide.

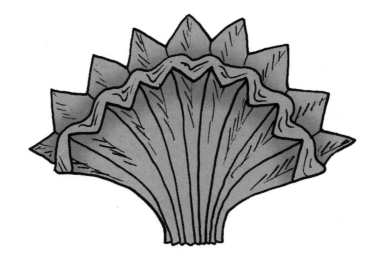

5. Securely hold the side with the single-folded edge and separate the two layers on the opposite side so they are fanned out.

Place in a glass or napkin ring to hold the bottom together.

NAPKIN RING WREATHS
Miniature 3″ grapevine wreaths are available at most craft supply stores - Decorate them with artificial fruits and berries, small bows, or acorns and tiny pine cones.

SNAKE RIVER LOG JAM

1. Start with flat napkin.

2. Fold in quarters with loose points up.

3. Roll first layer down from the top to the center.

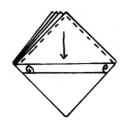

4. Roll the other three layers – stopping each one next to the last and roll up the bottom to meet the other four rolls.

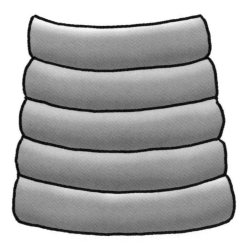

5. Fold right and left sides back and tuck one into the other forming a cylinder.

EXERCISE YOUR CREATIVITY!
Arrange any of the napkin folds that will lay flat on a plate – place any little item that you especially like on top.
For example:

Sea Shells	Pine Cones
River-Washed Rocks	Refrigerator Magnets
Toy Cars	Fresh Flowers
Miniature "Anythings"	Silk or Dried Flowers
Small Bunch of Herbs	Flags

A border of multi-shades of blue on this old tablecloth frames a dark blue plate with a crisp napkin folded into the "Fourth of July Fireworks". Clear lucite napkin rings add a sparkle and hold the accordion folds of the napkin in place. (See Page 48)

The "Air Force B-52" fold adapts very nicely to napkins that have a print in one corner. With most folds, the design would be upside-down. Hearts are pretty for Valentine's Day, but also look great with country décor. Here we go again – I found the darling heart-covered bowl, mugs and blue rimmed plates at flea markets and garage sales! (See Page 10)

122

The "Sun Valley Ski Cap" is truly seasonal with this red and green plaid napkin placed on a crisp white plate. My Mother painted the ceramic "family sleigh ride". A red candle and red poinsettia add just a touch of contrast. (See Page 128)

Can't you almost smell the apple pie? Invite some friends over for dessert and fold the napkins into "Blueridge Backpackers". Decorate with lots of snowmen and have a cozy evening. (See Page 18)

123

ST. LOUIS ARCH

1. Start with a flat napkin in diamond position.

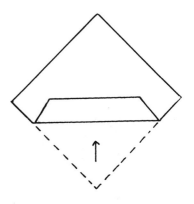

2. Starting at the bottom point, roll tightly on the diagonal all the way to the top point.

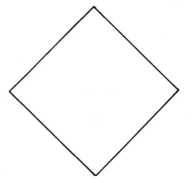

3. Tie a knot in center or leave it as is if fabric is heavy and doesn't tie easily.

- *Place on service plate circling a salad plate or soup bowl.*
- *Drape in a wine goblet.*
- *Circle a mug of coffee, hot chocolate or cup of soup.*
- *Place directly on the table above the plate.*

"CRAFTY" IDEA
Check your local craft stores for unfinished wooden
napkin rings. They can be stained or painted any
combination of colors, or turn your kids loose to
decorate them with non-toxic paints.

1. Start with flat napkin.

2. Fold in half with open edges at the top.

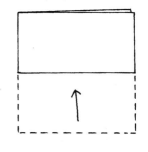

3. Roll from left side into the center.

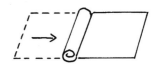

4. Hold roll securely and flip the whole thing over.

5. Roll remaining end into the center.

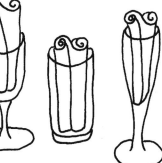

Place a note for someone special between the two rolls or stand the rolls on end in a glass.

Sun Valley Ski Cap

1. Start with flat napkin.

2. Fold in quarters with loose points down.

3. Fold up top layer.

4. Fold remaining three bottom layers up and inside the triangle.

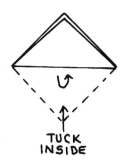

TUCK INSIDE

5. Bring top layer back down.

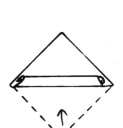

6. Roll from the bottom up to center creating a "cuff."

7. Fold right and left corners behind and tuck one inside the other to create "cap."

Note: The color or print on the wrong side of the napkin will be the color or print on the "cuff" of the cap.

TUCSON TEEPEE

1. Start with flat napkin.

2. Fold right and left sides into the center so they just meet.

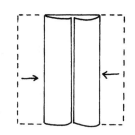

3. Fold each corner diagonally out from the center. (Hold the center down.)

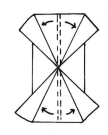

4. Roll the top half very tightly down to the center and roll the bottom half very tightly up to the center.

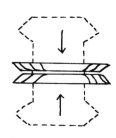

5. Fold the ends up to form the "poles" and flatten the middle to form the "teepee."

6. Cross the points to hold the "teepee" together.

Use a woven, striped napkin for an Indian effect.

BUYING TIP
For ease of folding, avoid paper napkins with a design only on part of the napkin. Also, fabric napkins that are "springy" and won't crease a little when folded probably won't work out well with most folds.

TWIN CITIES

1. Start with flat napkin.

2. Fold in half with open edges at the bottom.

3. Determine the center bottom point.

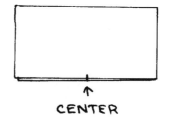

CENTER

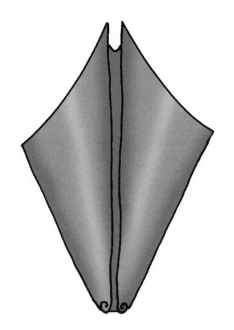

4. Start with bottom right corner and roll loosely toward center forming a cone shape.

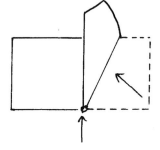

5. Do the same with left side.

Place it on a plate, stand it up in a tall glass, or slip it into a napkin ring.

U.S. ARMY CHEVRON

1. Start with flat napkin in diamond position.

2. Fold into triangle with points up.

3. Fold the bottom right and left points up to the top point.

4. Fold the bottom point up to the top.

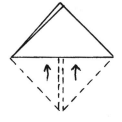

5. Bring right and left sides together and tuck one inside of the other to form a cylinder.

Don't forget to salute!!

U.S. POSTAL SERVICE

1. Start with flat napkin in diamond position.

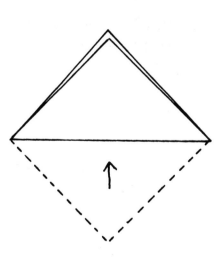

2. Fold into triangle with points up.

3. Fold right and left points in to meet at center of bottom edge.

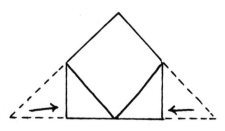

4. Fold right and left sides in again to just meet at the center.

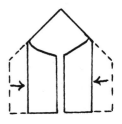

5. Fold lower part up to the base of the triangle.

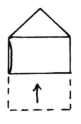

6. Fold the top triangle down to form an "envelope."

Neither rain, nor sleet, nor hail...

Yellowstone's
Old Faithful

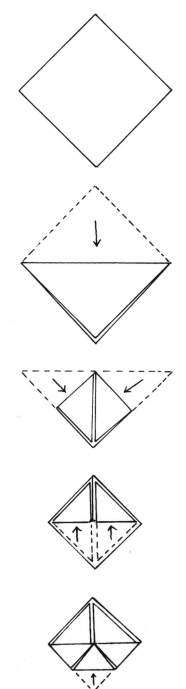

1. Start with flat napkin in diamond position.

2. Fold into triangle with points down.

3. Fold right and left points down to the bottom point.

4. Fold the two points you just placed at the bottom back up to center top.

5. Fold remaining bottom point up just to the center.

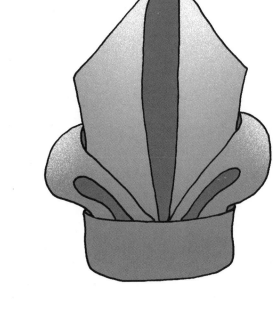

6. Fold this piece up again to center.

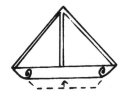

7. Fold this piece one more time so that it is folded on top of the upper triangle.

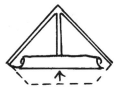

8. Flip over so smooth side is up.

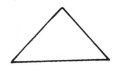

9. Tuck one side into the other to create a cylinder.

10. Turn napkin around and fold the loose points down and tuck them into the cuff.

Yosemite Campers

1. Start with flat napkin.

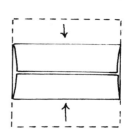

2. Fold the bottom up and the top down so they meet at the center.

3. Fold the top down to the bottom with the two folded edges at the bottom.

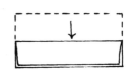

4. Fold the right and left ends down so they form a triangle at the top.

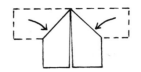

5. Flip the whole thing over.

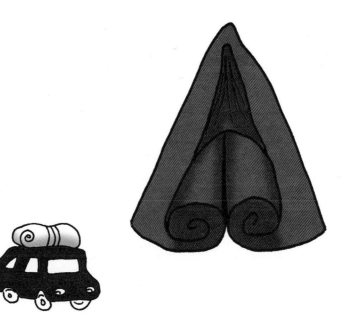

6. Roll up the "legs" to the bottom edge of the triangle.

7. Fold the rolls up to the center top – so they are alongside each other.

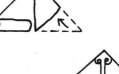

8. Turn the napkin over and stand it up so the "bedrolls" are on the bottom and the tent is shaped nicely above them.

A red bandana was perfect for the "Cheyenne Cowboy" fold. I used white paint on a small length of picket fence from the craft store to create a napkin ring. The pickets are strung together with wire that bends easily into a circle. A red checked tablecloth is always a nice basic for your linen collection. (See Page 36)

The "China Town Fan" stands up nicely on my Mother's dishes. Fresh daisies on the plate circle a bright yellow checked napkin. My parents brought the handmade copper and brass coffee service home from a trip to Mexico in the late 1950's. (See Page 40)

Cookies and lemonade taste better when served on old Pyrex restaurant-style dishes and coordinating glasses that I found at a flea market. The fold for the bright lemon colored napkins is the "Holland, Michigan Tulip". The summery latticework tablecloth is from the early 1940's. (See Page 66)

These cute plastic ice cream dishes are borrowed from friend Virginia Whitmore's "Grandma's Hope Chest". The "All-American Ice Cream Cone" fold is perfect for the cool pastel plaid napkin. (See Page 12)

Placemats

Copy the designs on the following pages onto 8½″ × 14″ plain or colored copy paper and let your kids or grandkids color them. Let them help fold the napkins too. Their involvement and pride in decorating the tabletop will bring the whole family to the table!

Copy designs, cut and paste your choice, then recopy and color them.

146

147

Theme Tables

Theme tables have become very popular and can be as little or as much work as you want them to be. Use your imagination! Look around your house – you already have many items that can be used to set the stage. Try houseplants (real or artificial), figurines, collectibles, candles, birdhouses, baskets, pine cones, etc. Just plan ahead and make sure whatever you use is clean – bugs and dirt are not very appetizing at the table.

GARDEN PARTY

Start with a green or garden motif tablecloth. Purchase inexpensive three or four inch flower pots and paint a repeat design from the tablecloth or some simple flowers on the pots with acrylic paints. If you don't want to paint, try applying stickers. Fold a dark green napkin into a triangle and tuck it into the pot so the points hang over the edge and create a "leaf" effect. Fold a floral print napkin, or one that matches the tablecloth, into the "Pottstown Peony" and place it in the center of the "leaves". Purchase small pots of live flowers to give each guest at the end of the party – but first use them as a centerpiece by placing them all together in a flat basket in the center of the table. (When I did this party, we used the printed napkin for our laps and at the end of the meal we had fun trying different napkin folds with the green napkin. It was a great conversation-extender!) A pretty variation of this theme would be to use birdhouses as centerpieces and small pots of herbs instead of the flowers.

BEACH OR POOL PARTY

Use a bright colored tablecloth of plastic or fabric – sunny yellow, fresh lime, hot pink or cool tangerine would be nice choices. The napkins can be striped, checked, floral or plain, as long as they coordinate. The "Moon Over Miami" or "Palm Beach Palm" folds would be great – or try a fold that will stand up at each service place – this will dress up the spot until the person arrives with their plate full of food. For a quick centerpiece place any plant you already have into a child's sand pail. If you want something more dramatic, add some fresh flowers to the plant. Small water vials can be purchased from your florist or local craft supply to keep the flowers fresh throughout the entire party. Strings of white mini lights can be wound around 9´ silk garlands of ivy. I then tape or tie on silk flowers and drape the lights all around the deck or patio. I found all sorts of wooden precut hearts, flowers, birdhouses, etc. at my craft store. We painted them, drilled holes in the top, and tied them on the ivy and light strands with raffia (or you could use ribbon) at about 6″ intervals. This is a great way to develop your basic theme.

BE MY VALENTINE?

This theme begins with a plain red tablecloth. Purchase large white doilies to use as placemats. Make sure they are larger than the plates you will be using so they show around the edges. Small 4″ round doilies can be placed under the glasses. Fresh pink or red and white flowers are wonderful as a center-piece. An alternative to flowers could be a "bouquet" of paper hearts attached to wire "stems" and stuck into a pretty pot of ivy. I used a heart-shaped cookie cutter to make hearts from sliced beets to garnish the salads. Many magazines feature fun recipes in February with a "heart" theme. Search your local stores, garage sales, and flea markets for pretty red dishes, bowls and platters. Milk glass accent dishes are striking with the red tablecloth too. Use a frilly napkin folded into the "Boston Tea Party" or the "U.S. Postal Service" folds.

FOLLOW YOUR TEAM PARTY

This theme can be used for any sporting event – just start with your team's colors. Use rubber stamps with non-toxic inks and non-toxic fabric paints to decorate a tablecloth or placemats. If your favorite team is well known, you may find paper or plastic tableware with their colors and logo. I have found sturdy reusable plastic trays, bowls and chip dip dishes with a generic football, soccer or basketball theme. Napkins folded into the "Blueridge Backpackers" can be tucked into a basket and placed near the food so they are convenient and ready to use.

Kid's Parties

AUTO RACING

Use a bright red plastic tablecloth and black and white checked paper plates and cups. Fold a red paper napkin into the "LA Freeway" fold and place a small race car on the "freeway lanes" as a favor. A styrofoam base with black and white checked flags would be a great centerpiece.

AIRPLANES

Use the "Air Force B52" fold and look for paper plates with a related design. Once you have found the plates, color-coordinate the rest of the table. Use glue or silly putty to affix an airplane to the end of a 10″ wooden dowel. Secure the dowel in a styrofoam base for the center of the table. Using 8″ squares of colored plastic wrap or foil, poke the center of the square into the styrofoam. Cover the top and sides of the base this way. Make sure the base is large enough that the weight of the plane will not topple it over.

CAMPING, HIKING, OR SCOUTING

Either the "Blueridge Backpacker" or the "Tucson Teepee" fold would work well for this theme. Make an 18″ teepee for the center of the table from sticks found in the yard and fake "suede" cloth found at your local fabric store. Cake decorating shops are a good source for little plastic figures to decorate a cake top or cupcakes. As an alternate centerpiece use a basket filled with pine cones or an arrangement made with pine boughs to add a wonderful woodsy scent.

TEA PARTY

The key to this theme is to use beautiful pastel colors with a pretty floral motif. Coordinate the tablecloth, napkins, paper plates and add a pretty centerpiece. The focal point could be a vase of flowers or stand a doll on a styrofoam base and attach fresh or silk flowers from the waist down to create her "skirt". Fold the napkin into an "Oahu Orchid" and place the center of the folded napkin into a glass so the points create a "skirt" over the rim of the glass. Place a small doll in the center of the napkin as a favor.